The Holistic Guide To Cold-Calling

A Step-By-Step Guide To Help You Grow Your Business

Simone Laraway

This book is dedicated to my Ikigai

"As soon as you take these first small steps, your anxiety will disappear, and you will achieve a pleasant flow in the activity you're doing." — Hector Garcia Puigcerver

Copyright © 2021

Simone Laraway.

All rights reserved. This book or any portion thereof may not be reproduced or used in any manner whatsoever without the express written permission of the author except for the use of brief quotations in a book review.

First printing, 2021.

ISBN: 9798739348982

simone@thevocalbureau.com

www.thevocalbureau.com

Cover Design – Melli M Designs

TABLE OF CONTENTS

INTRODUCTION	6
THE AIM	8
STEP 1 - WHO?	15
STEP 2 – WHAT DO YOU DO?	19
STEP 3 - WHO YOU DO IT FOR	29
STEP 4 –WHY?	32
STEP 5 –YOUR OPENING LINES	37
STEP 6 -WHO YOU GONNA CALL?	39
POSSIBLE OUTCOMES	42
STEP 7 - PUTTING IT TOGETHER	55
CHALLENGE TIME!	59
STEP 8 - ORGANISATION	61
STEP 9 - MAKE THE TIME	69
STEP 10 - FINDING LEADS	72
STEP 11 – YOUR TOOL KIT	79
STEP 12 - WHAT MAKES A GOOD CALL?	82

STEP 13 - HOW TO SAY IT	95
VOCAL CARE	100
STEP 14 – MENTAL PREPARATION	102
STEP 15 - YOUR FIRST CALL & BEYOND	104
ARGHHHHH – NOW WHAT?	108
TROUBLESHOOTING	112
CONCLUSION	116
RESOURCES	120

INTRODUCTION

Welcome to my world of cold-calling. With over 20 years of experience doing new business calling, consulting, and vocal coaching, I want to help make cold-calling the enjoyable experience it can be, rather than the chore most people think it is.

I wrote this book to help you use the phone with confidence. To show you how to build your business or career by connecting and introducing yourself to people, not targets, leads, or prospects, but real people who might benefit from your call.

It is for anyone who needs to start building their business using the telephone as part of their strategy.

You might have your own business and have no idea how to talk about it. Or perhaps you want to create new opportunities and are unsure how to do this. You might not have set up your business yet but have a seed of an idea and want to learn how to make that idea bloom.

I encourage you to view your new business not merely as a database but as an organic, living thing that needs love, nurture and patience to help it grow.

I'm passionate about cold-calling and the opportunities it can create. I hope to fill you with a sense of pride when you put down the phone after a good conversation and the glow you get when you create new business opportunities.

This step-by-step guide is about making cold-calling an enjoyable and practical part of your new business programme.

The Aim

This book aims to give you the tools you need to build your business constructively and logically by good old-fashioned talking!

By the end of this book, you'll be able to:

- Define yourself/ your business
- Distil what you do into a "phone-ready" sentence or two
- Know who it is you need to talk to
- How to find them
- Organise your new business effectively
- Get on the phone & talk about your business to help you create new opportunities
- Have a "phone-ready" marketing toolkit
- Pick up the phone rather than relying on email
- View the phone as a source of opportunity and growth, not something that will bring you out in a cold sweat every time you go to pick it up.

New business calling is not a quick fix but takes patience, time, and perseverance which will reap the rewards for years if tended properly.

I've included lined pages for you to jot down and scribble any ideas you might have along the way.

So let us begin.

The first lockdown was undoubtedly a wake-up call for me. Like many others, work and home life collided unceremoniously, and after a great deal of frantic, chaotic scrambling to find a new "norm", we all found ways to juggle and find that new work-life balance.

One sunny afternoon during that first lockdown, I found a rare moment where I had some space to think and breathe.

I had been listening to the audiobook, *Ikigai – The Japanese Secret to a Long and Happy Life,* by Francesc Miralles and Hector Garcia. Now, if you are unfamiliar with the notion of Ikigai, it has various translations but essentially means the search for your purpose.

It got me thinking about whether I had indeed found my purpose. Was I living my Ikigai? And if I did uncover my Ikigai, then could I find true balance?

Don't get me wrong, I was teaching singing and voice online and had a couple of new business clients, but I felt that I wasn't reaching my potential; I wanted to help more people with the skills I'd developed and my business just felt disjointed.

For years, I knew there must be a way to combine my voice coaching with my new business development skills, but life and work got in the way. I never quite got around to making it happen, so the ideas just sat there simmering on the backburner.

I decided to take this little pocket of peace and address the questions swirling about in my mind.

Could I discover my Ikigai? And would I be able to apply it to my life?

I have always loved voice, singing, and helping others unlock their potential. I am also very passionate about cold-calling and helping businesses grow.

So, with my cup of tea in hand, I started to let my mind wander and think about my business life; what was my Ikigai? Was I living and breathing what I love to do? And how could I help more people?

With an enormous sheet of paper, I took a deep breath and dived in. Collating all my various half-used notebooks with half-finished ideas and musings, I gathered my pens, sticky notes, and glitter. I just started to scribble, doodle, write and express how I saw my skills and experiences (the good, the bad and the ugly!) and my hopes for the future. I kept working to uncover the connections that I knew were there.

After a good sleep and talking to my family about my discoveries, The Vocal Bureau was born.

From there, everything began to fall into place, but enough about me, let's get you started on your journey.

"Let's start at the very beginning, it's a very good place to start"- Julie Andrews- The Sound of Music

STEP 1
WHO?

You may already have your business in place and need to refresh your new business efforts.

On the other hand, perhaps you are a new start-up, and you don't know where to begin. Maybe you have an idea of a business but haven't got the name yet.

The fact is we all need to start somewhere and as Julie says, starting at the beginning seems a very good place to start.

The first and most crucial step is to know yourself.

Know **WHO** you are:

- Can you define yourself and your company succinctly?
- Do you have a company name?
- Are you an individual offering your services/skills?
- Are you part of a partnership or team?
- Do you have the seed of an idea?

- Are you an established business but need a refresh & refocus?

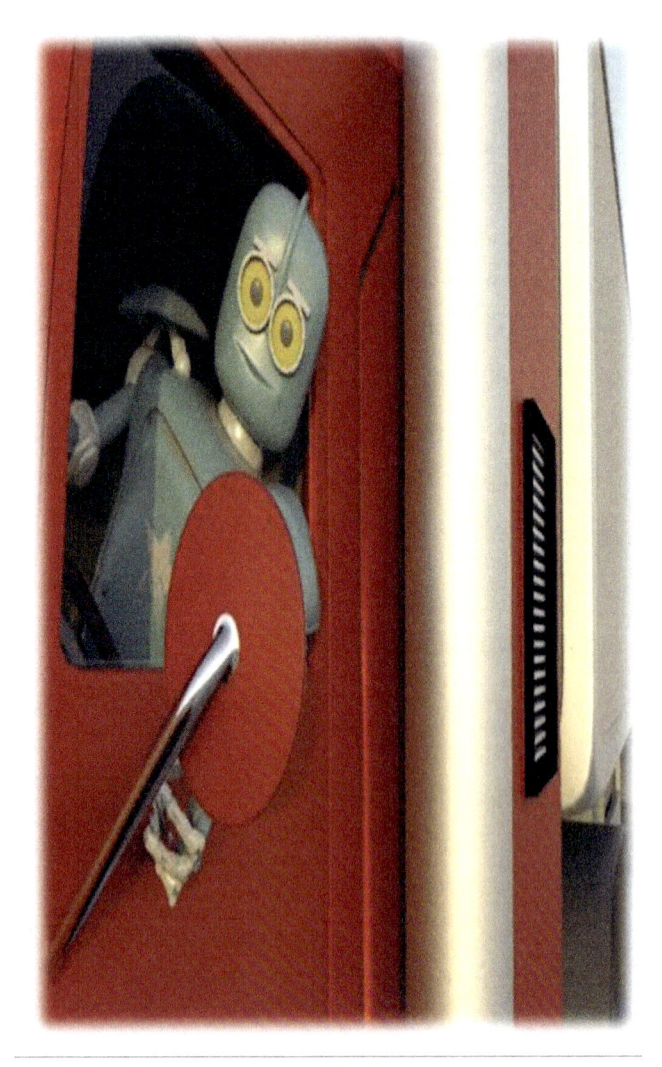

STEP 2
WHAT DO YOU DO?

The second step is to know what it is you do. You need to confidently sum up what you do in a sentence or two.

Know **WHAT** you do – What is it that you/your company offers.

- What services do you offer?
- What is it that you provide?

To communicate well, you need to know **WHO** you are and **WHAT** you do. Not just on the phone but through your branding, social media engagement, and marketing materials that you share with the world.

When you call, people are busy, and you have seconds to grab their attention, so be clear and concise about:

- Who you are
- What you do
- Why you are calling

If this is something you feel you can already do, you can skip ahead to **STEP THREE**.

However, if the thought of this brings you out in a cold sweat and your head is filled with "Um's" and "Ah well's" and can't define yourself or your company succinctly, then let's get stuck in.

"Knowing yourself is the beginning of all wisdom"
Aristotle

WHO ARE YOU & WHAT DO YOU DO?

I invite you to get creative here and immerse yourself in this process.

Take a big piece of paper, write down the words, or draw the pictures that spring to mind when you start thinking about your company. I'm old school and like getting tactile to help me think!

Create a mood board, take a walk, whatever you can think of to get your brain fired up so that you can discover the heart and essence of your company/business/brand or you as an individual.

Remember you are looking to distil yourself/ your company into a couple of sentences.

- Who you are, and what you do?

Below are some questions to help get you started:

- Who Are You?
- What is it that you do?
- What are your hopes and dreams?
- Do you have a vision or big picture?
- What are your skills & talents?
- Do you have any awards, accomplishments, or accolades?
- Who do you do it for?

- Do you already have clients?
- Any failures that have given you insight on how to succeed?
- Do you have your branding in place already?
- Are you starting from scratch?
- What's your history?

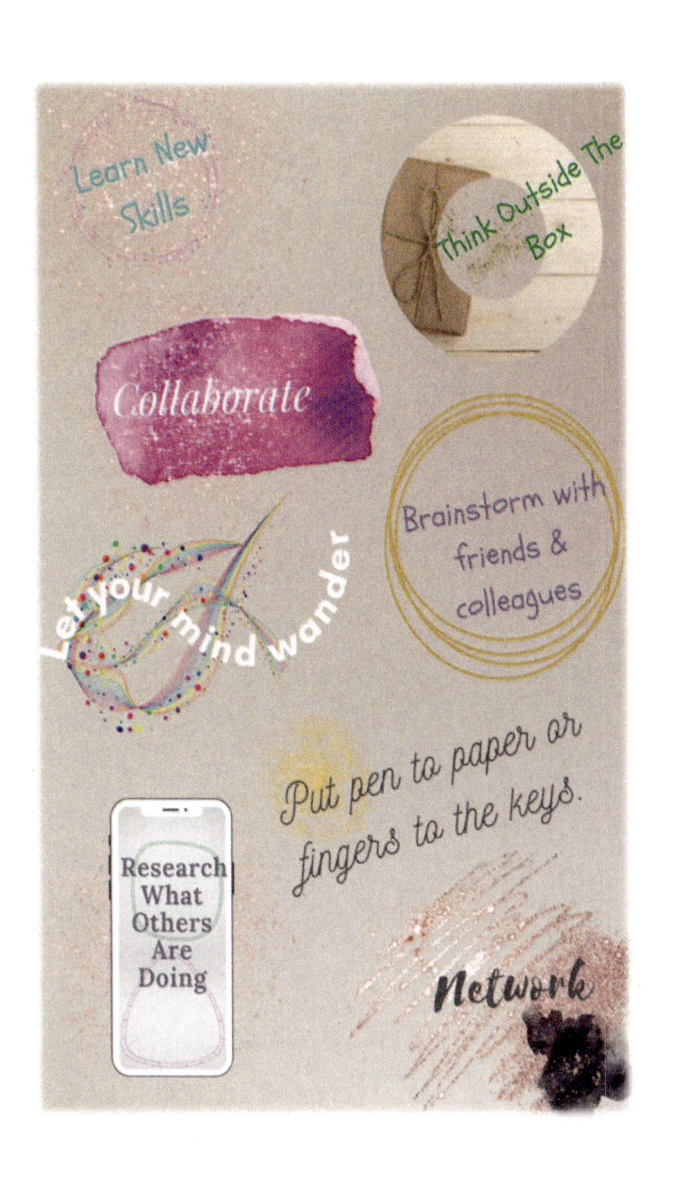

- Learn New Skills
- Think Outside The Box
- Collaborate
- Let your mind wander
- Brainstorm with friends & colleagues
- Research What Others Are Doing
- Put pen to paper or fingers to the keys.
- Network

Don't forget that we all have stories, so you might also want to write about how you got to this point in your journey.

Whatever you choose to do, your aim is to sum up your company in a sentence or two. **WHO** are you, and **WHAT** do you do?

Jot your sentence down:

YOU WILL NEED THIS FOR YOUR SCRIPT CREATION

Hopefully, you will have arrived at something that looks like this:

> *We are (company name), and we (whatever it is you do)*
>
> *I am a (what it is you are) and I (what is it you do)*

You now have the first step towards your script creation, and the first part of your script will look something like this:

> *My name is (YOUR NAME), and I am calling from (Your WHO and WHAT sentence goes here).*

It doesn't seem much, but LESS IS MORE, trust me.

"Simplicity is the ultimate sophistication."

Leonardo da Vinci.

STEP 3
WHO YOU DO IT FOR

This section of the script development is where you can toot your own horn.

If you are a brand new business with no clients or experience, this stage can be tricky.

It might be best to say **Who** you are, **What** you do, and go straight in with your **Why**. (We will come onto this shortly.)

If you are an established business with clients and case studies, you have an extra line to add to your script. It is time to name drop and add in **Who** you do it for.

Your sentence will look something like this:

> *We are (company name) and we (whatever it is you do). We're working with the likes of (Name Drop – A maximum of three)*
>
> *I am (your name), and I (whatever it is you do) and I'm working with the likes of (Name Drop – A maximum of three)*

Or you can switch it around a little:

> *We/I are/am (company name), and we/I work with (Name Drop – A maximum of three) and help them (whatever it is you do)*

Or something slightly different:

> *I'm calling from (Company name), and we're the agency/company behind or responsible for – insert your impressive piece of work here.*

It is essential to prioritise your new business efforts when you have something of note to talk about. It will help you stand out from the crowd, keep your calling fresh, and keep your mind engaged.

If you have live campaigns or work out there in the real world, you need to pick up the phone. For example, perhaps you're a packaging design agency and have just helped a major brand relaunch, and the products are on shelf.

Perhaps you are an events agency, and your event has had lots of press coverage.

Maybe you have just won an award, or you've just had an article written about you or your innovations. Perhaps you've just won a new client.

Whatever the situation, live work is a beautiful tool in your toolkit. (More about toolkits shortly).

It's exciting to talk about things that are happening right now. This will impact your call, not only to give you something new to talk about, but also the person on the other end of the phone will hear the pride and excitement in your voice.

It gives you an extra opportunity to connect. They might well have seen the product on shelf, or read about your event, or seen the press coverage you achieved for your client. All this helps to build good relationships on the phone and gives credence to your work and why you are calling.

So, as my old Granny would say, "don't be shy about coming forward!" (But don't be pushy)

Have faith that your work will speak for itself.

STEP 4
WHY?

We have our first three steps, **Who**, **What** and **Who.** Now we must consider the **WHY**.

We need to think about why we are calling.

- What is it you want to achieve?
- What is the reason for the call?
- Ask yourself what your objective is

You cannot simply call someone to introduce yourself and not know why; it would be a bizarre and awkward call!

It's important to get to the why of the call quickly. People do not have time to listen to you waffle.

The following are examples of what it is you might be trying to achieve:

Set up a meeting/appointment be it online or face to face

You are trying to sell a specific product or service

Arranging a demo

Building awareness of your brand & you simply want to capture email addresses

Inviting someone to a webinar/conference

You don't have a contact and are simply researching to find the correct person

So, establish your **Why**, and we are on our way to making our first call.

STEP 5
YOUR OPENING LINES

The script starts as a simple equation:

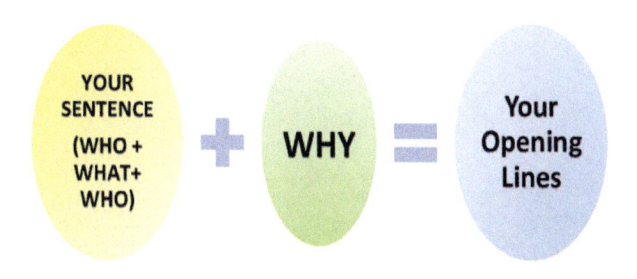

YOUR SENTENCE (WHO + WHAT + WHO) + **WHY** = **Your Opening Lines**

Simplicity is critical because it keeps everything clear in your head, and it is also apparent to the person what the reason for the call is.

Now that we know what we need to say, we need to consider something vital: **The Who!**

No fun in rehearsing a play if you have no audience on opening night!

STEP 6
WHO YOU GONNA CALL?

So, you know **Who you are**, **What you do**, **Who you do it for**, and **Why you are calling.**

The next step is to consider **Who are you going to call**?

During your brainstorming session, or even before, you may have identified who you want to connect with. What sector you want to work in, where your strengths and experiences lie, and what sort of organisations would benefit from your offering.

You may even know which people within those companies would be the right contacts. If you do, bravo, you can move on to the next section - **Possible Outcomes.**

However, some of you may well not have a Scooby-Doo clue about who it is you need to speak to or how to go about talking to them.

To discover your **Who** ask yourself the following questions:

- Who could benefit from what I offer?
- Who needs my services and skills?
- What sectors would I fit? Financial, Home Furnishings, Days Out, IT etc.
- Do I have any relevant experience/training I can bring to the table in specific sectors, business types?
- What contacts do I already have?
- Do I have anyone to make introductions/give recommendations on my behalf?
- What departments would be most appropriate? (i.e., if you offer training courses in voice, then HR/Training might be an excellent place to start)
- Do I have specific sector experience? And can that translate into other sectors?
- Am I a specialist in a particular field?
- If you have them, who are my competitors working with?

Suppose you're a marketing agency with a specialism in marine marketing. In that case, buying a list of HR managers in pet foods will not yield many (if any) results and would leave you feeling deflated and the people you're calling perplexed.

However, if you are a packaging design agency specialising in FMCG, buying a list/researching leads for Brand Directors in FMCG would be a good fit. You would have a much higher success rate of having relevant conversations and building your opportunities.

Remember, cold-calling takes time and energy! Identifying the people who need your services will help avoid wasting your time and theirs.

Let's not get bogged down with the leads themselves, as we'll cover this later on in **Step 10**.

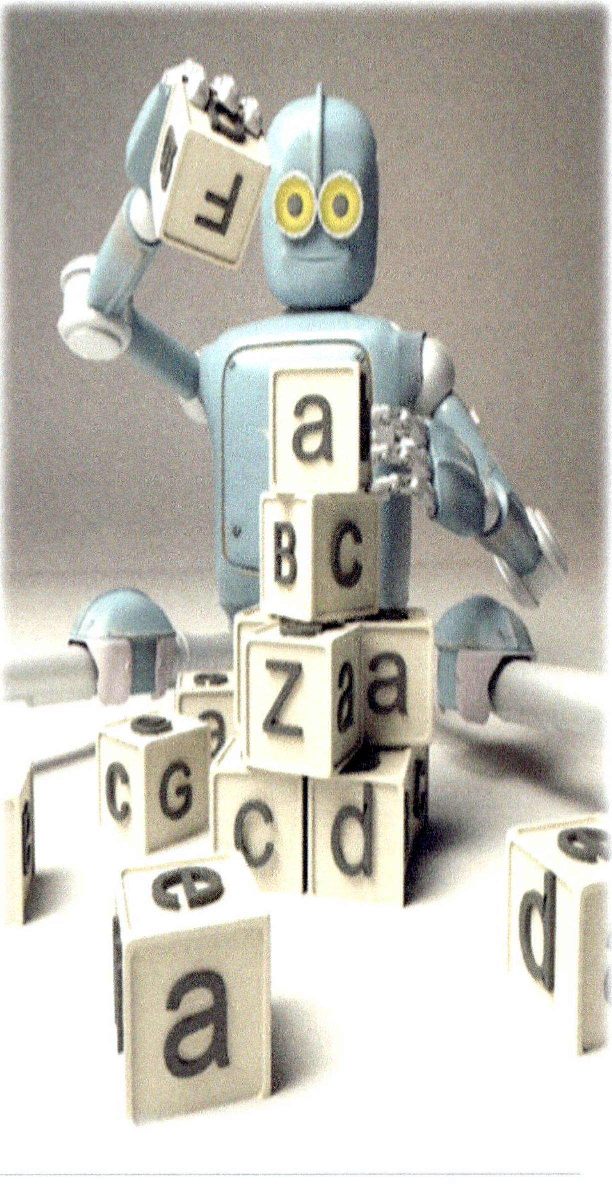
a
B C
Z a
c G
c d
a
d

POSSIBLE OUTCOMES

I know you are itching to pick up that phone to kick start your new business, but we need to address several other issues.

We've focused on what you have to say. Now we need to consider something equally important, what the other person might say back to you.

There are three answers you may well encounter:

THE YES

Obviously, the response we want is YES. This is the reason we are picking up the phone in the first place. We want to create new opportunities, and a YES is a step closer to that.

In this situation, you would say something along the lines of:

"Perfect. Can I take your email address, and I'll send you a diary invite for our call/demo" (whatever it is you have agreed on).

THE MAYBE

MAYBE's happen for different reasons, and you have to develop your gut feeling here and learn patience.

A MAYBE could turn into a client quickly, be a slow burner, or just someone being polite and not wanting to say no to you.

Below are a couple of ways you could deal with your MAYBE:

You have piqued someone's interest, but they don't want to commit straight away and want to ponder some more. Your response:

"Great, could I perhaps take your email, and I'll send you some examples of our work."

Take their email and then say that you will call them again in a few days to see what they think.

Another scenario could be that it's just not the right time. This could be due to budgets or other business issues, such as projects, procurement, staff changes etc. They could see the potential of your offering and would like you to stay in touch.

Your response:

"Well, in that case, would it be ok if I sent you our details and get back in touch."

Send them an email and make a note to call again when you said you would.

There is also the possibility that your MAYBE might be a NO in disguise, and the person is just too nice to say it. In this scenario, you can respond with one of the answers above (whichever suits the call), and you'll find out in due course whether it is a true MAYBE or not.

THE NO!

Just because someone says NO at that moment does not mean that the call is a lost cause.

NO could be a MAYBE in disguise and, therefore, a potential YES. So don't always take a NO at face value.

NO's come in different shapes and sizes, and it would be impossible to list them all here, but I've tried to think of common NO's, and when you get on the phone and start making the calls, you will develop a sense of where opportunities lie and when you are heading down a dead end.

Some examples:

- **NO, sorry, I'm moving roles next month.** In this scenario, your NO is an opportunity to speak to a new person coming into the position who might be very interested to hear what you have to say. Don't forget to ask where the person is moving to as their new role might be relevant!
- **NO, we do not outsource but do everything in house.** In this case, ask if they ever outsource the odd project, and if they do, say great, and ask if you can send your details and try to stay in touch.
- **NO, we already work with someone.** You could ask whether there is a review process and if you could get in touch when they are looking to review/renew contracts
- **NO, we have to go through procurement.** This is a bit of a minefield but worth jumping through the hoops to get on a procurement list. (It is not always easy, and you need to use your judgement).

- **NO, we have no budgets.** Ask whether they have an annual review. When do they review their budgets?

You will sometimes face a NO when you've not even finished your opening gambit. It is essential to listen to what the person is saying to you.

Listen for the clues:

- Do they sound distracted?
- What do you hear in the background?

They may interrupt before you've finished and say, *"sorry, not interested,"* and put the phone down.

You may have called at a bad time, and they are not listening but simply want to get you off the phone to meet that deadline or get onto a meeting.

If you feel that you didn't get the opportunity to engage with the person, all is not lost. Take the pressure off and say, "oh well," and simply call them another time armed with the information you just gathered about them.

Believe it or not, that call has given you insight so that you can adapt your approach next time. Just make notes about their manner and tone of voice and anything else you think you can use when you next approach them.

For example - If they were curt and snappy, next time, go in and say, ***"Hello, I'm so and so, and I'm going to be really quick and say that we would like to (whatever your goal is) because (insert what you do here).***

PATIENCE IS A VIRTUE

Another possible outcome is where you do not get through to the person at all. For example, you may have their direct dial, but they are constantly on voicemail.

Keep trying, but **NEVER** leave a voicemail because you have no idea how your message will be received or if it has even been heard. You have also gained no information about that person.

I called someone for over a year who was constantly on voicemail. Then, one day, out of the blue, luck or synchronicity was on my side, and the person picked up. I tried my best not to sound surprised and carried on as usual. So be patient.

GATEKEEPERS

Another situation is that the decision-maker you want has a PA or Secretary, and you will have little chance of getting through.

There are different takes on this. Some say that you don't speak to the PA, don't give your name or details. However, the PA is a person too. They will get to know your voice and get annoyed if you keep calling but refuse to let them help you.

In my experience, if there is a gatekeeper, just be honest about why you are calling. Ask for advice on how best to achieve your WHY.

You can also ask if there might be anyone else in the organisation you could speak to. Always be courteous, and don't forget that sometimes the gatekeeper is the person who presents ideas to the decision-maker.

However, this is an area where you will learn through trial and error. There is no definitive answer.

ASK OPEN QUESTIONS

If you've received a NO or a MAYBE, you must try to ask open questions. What, When, and Who are good words to use to help you engage with the person for longer to keep your conversation going. You could ask some of the following questions:

- When would be a good time for them to meet? And add on, "I'm thinking the week of... if that suits you?"
- When do they review?
- What do you do in the way of...?
- When would be a better time to call?
- Can you send them further details and ask if you can follow up in a few days
- Ask if it would be ok to take their email address and send them some details?
- Who would be the best person to speak to about...?

Now that we know our possible outcomes, we can develop our script fully.

STEP 7
PUTTING IT TOGETHER

Step seven is about putting it together to create your script.

Your opening lines would look something like this:

> **Good Morning/Afternoon, could I speak to** (name of the person).
>
> My name is **(Name),** and I am calling from **(Who & What sentence),** and I was hoping that I could **(Why sentence)**

If you have clients/live work or something to brag about, then you could use the following sentence:

> **Good Morning/Afternoon, could I speak to** (name of the person).
>
> My name is **(Name),** and I am calling from **(Who & What sentence), (We work with Name Drop),** and I was hoping that I could **(Why Sentence)**

So that it feels a little more coherent, let's put our opening lines into (loosely fictitious) case studies so that you can see how the script works in action.

> *Naomi is a designer who creates emotive designs for the charity sector. She has set up a company called Emotive Designs. She has worked for well-known charities but feels that her new business needs a kick start. She knows new business is something that she needs to tackle but has been putting it off!*
>
> **She would say something along the lines of:**
>
> "Good morning my name is Naomi Stephens, and I'm calling from Emotive Designs.
>
> We specialise in creating poignant designs for the charity sector and work with **charity names.** I was hoping to introduce myself and our work, and wondered if you had any time in the next few weeks to arrange a zoom meeting?"

Charlie is a health & lifestyle coach and has created a training course for corporate wellness, focused on employees working from home.

His script would look something like this:

"Good morning my name is Charlie Smith, and I specialise in corporate wellness.

I've created a corporate wellness course for home workers, and was hoping to introduce myself, and wondered if you had any time in the next few weeks to arrange a zoom meeting?"

Anya is a crafter and makes handmade organic soap. She has been selling online but wants to reach out to gift shops across her region.

She would say something along the lines of:

"Good morning my name is Anya, and I create handmade organic soap.

I love your shop and wondered if I could arrange a time to pop in and show you my work?"

ADDRESS: (Writing these things in are useful because your brain will freeze)
NAME:
EMAIL:
PHONE:
WEB ADDRESS:

SCRIPT

(When you don't have a contact) Good Morning/ Afternoon could you tell me who is responsible for (whatever department/job title you think is appropriate for you)

(When you do have a name) Good Morning/ Afternoon could I speak to (name of the person).

My name is (Your Name) and I am calling from (Your WHO & WHAT sentence), (We work with NAME DROP) and I was hoping that I could (YOUR WHY SENTENCE)

IF YES – Perfect. Can I take your email address and I will send you a diary invite (or whatever you have agreed upon) and a link to our website/relevant marketing materials.

If NO/Maybe – ASK open questions:
- Ask if a date further along in the diary would be better for them?
- Ask whether you can call back another time later in the year?
- Ask if you can send them further details and say you will follow up in a week or so
- Would it be ok if I took your email address and sent you some details across? When would be a good time to get in touch again? Do you think...? Can you recommend? Etc

CHALLENGE TIME!

Set your stop-watch and see how long it takes you to say your script. You're aiming for under 20 seconds but are also trying to sound relaxed!

I don't want you to sound too polished and slick. I want you to sound natural and relaxed. (Easier said than done!) Keep practising until you feel comfortable and you're not floundering about, adding Um's and Ah's.

STEP 8
ORGANISATION

Creating Your New Business Database

We've talked about potential outcomes to your calls, so the next step is to consider how you will organise those conversations.

Nurture each call even if you're rejected several times or can't get through; You need to persist. The way to be consistent in your persistence is to be organised.

You must capture information and have a foolproof system so that you call your contact when you say you are going to, and don't call people who have said they don't want to be called!

Take notes that will help you remember the call you had with them. Good note-taking keeps the person you spoke to fresh in your mind and enables you to build a connection, even when you call back a year down the line!

You need to contact people when you say you are going to and remember to record any valuable information. For example:

- When do they review their suppliers? Update their IT? When is their recruitment cycle?
- When will the person you need be back from maternity leave? A new person is starting; someone else is leaving. Someone has been ill etc.
- The company is restructuring, and they have a new CEO.
- There are relevant articles in the press.
- Record anything unusual about your conversation. Did you talk about anything personal that did not relate to the call?
- Record whatever you feel is relevant to you and your business.

What System Should You Use?

If you are a small business and it's just you on the phone, and you only have a small number of people to contact, you do not need a system with bells and whistles. Just something simple where you can record your information.

When I first started, I used a large folder with A4 sheets of paper and dividers with the months on. Not sophisticated, but it did the job! So, I made my notes and popped the sheet of paper into the month they needed a callback, and eh voila! My new business database at my fingertips.

However, today we are recording email addresses and digital information such as links to the websites and LinkedIn profiles, so you must have a digital database.

If you deal with large amounts of data and perhaps are part of a team, you need a robust CRM (Customer Relationship Management) system. I've learned the hard way that there is nothing worse than calling someone who informs you that someone in your company has just called them! It's cringeworthy, and you've potentially jeopardised a relationship with someone. Plus, it just makes you and your company look unprofessional and a little incompetent.

I will leave this for you to choose and explore. I have listed several effective CRMs at the back of the book that I've used in the past.

There are many systems out there that would help keep you on top of your information, and only you know how tech-savvy you are and what you need from your CRM.

What Will Be In Your Database?

Once you start calling, your leads will begin to fall into different categories:

GOAL – You achieved your **Why** – Booked that appointment, demo, telephone meeting etc. GO YOU!!

HOTS – You feel there is an excellent opportunity. The person has asked you to call back to discuss taking things further. You just know it's a **HOT** one.

WARMS – Good conversations which may lead to something.

CULTIVATE – Your NO's and some MAYBE's would fall into this category. They've shown a mild interest. They've said not at the moment, but please do keep in touch. These are the "You Never Know" ones. They are your slow burners or were NO's that you think could be a MAYBE.

NO's & NOT SPOKEN TO – Ones you feel are a dead end and those you are constantly trying to get hold of.

COLD CALLS – Fresh Leads that you've not yet called.

GOAL

HOTS

Warms

Cultivate

NO's and not spoken to

Cold Calls

Graphic design by Melli M Designs

STEP 9
Make The Time

It is very easy to procrastinate and find that the week/month has slipped by and you've not done any calling.

- Set a specific time each week to do your calling tasks.
- Prepare and organise your callbacks

How much time you assign is your choice. You can set aside a whole day, two half days, or do an hour or two each day. It depends on the practicalities of how you are going to fit your calling into your working week. If you do your calls correctly and target the right people, your new business calling can amount to as little as 3-4 hours a week.

So, choose a specific time, a morning or afternoon slot, and put it in your diary. Do not answer emails or calls if they are not related to your new business activity.

- Be strict and focus exclusively on your new business development.
- Commit to getting on the phone and not allow any distraction

STEP 10
FINDING LEADS

With your script and CRM in place, we are nearly there. All we need to do now is fill your database with the right contacts.

You know what sector, companies and people would be interested in you and how you can help them, but how do you find them?

Connect to people you have worked or work with to create "soft" opportunities. These will hopefully convert to clients more quickly than cold calls.

Do not be proud! Get on the phone and call colleagues, friends, family, and any acquaintance you think could benefit from your service. The bonus of this is that you'll get the opportunity to practise talking about your business offering and using your script.

Explore your contacts, mine any networks of which you might be a member.

Ask people to recommend you. Word of mouth is a great way to start building your business. Use any resources you can think of which will help to boost your profile.

Once you have your "soft" list, you can move on to building a list of cold contacts.

There are various ways to do this depending upon your services. Ask yourself:

- How much of your business needs to come from cold-calling?
- What is your budget?
- Who do you want to connect with?

The first way is by picking up the phone and doing it the old-fashioned way!

Let's imagine you have a list of fifty companies with their phone numbers but no contact names.

In this situation, you would say the following sentence:

Good Morning/Afternoon, could you tell me who is responsible for (whatever department/job title you think is appropriate for you)

Get your information, put the phone down and move on to your next call. When you have called all the companies, you will have your list of names to call on another calling day.

NB: You may be in a situation where the switchboard simply will not give out that information. If so, simply move on and perhaps do some online research.

Some companies might not hold names on the switchboard and put you through to the department. You can dig around to find the right person. However, this can take up precious time, and you may or may not find the information you need.

Other ways of finding leads include:

- Purchasing your leads - Some companies will create lists for you with the decision-maker, telephone numbers, email addresses etc., and this saves you time on research.
- Do you own online research using resources such as LinkedIn
- Use a resource, such as Fiverr, to help you build data and do the research for you.

What leads you need to find is influenced by several factors:

- Who are you targeting?
- Are you in a niche market?
- Are you doing B2B or B2C calling?
- What time do you have for finding leads?
- How many calls do you want to make?
- Do you have a budget to pay someone to source leads? Or to buy ready done lists?

At the back of this book, I have listed some lead sources I use and have used. However, there are many, and it is up to you to research and work out which leads suit your needs best.

CTPS - Corporate Telephone Preference Service

The Corporate Telephone Preference Service, or CTPS, lists organisations such as limited companies and public limited companies who have registered their wish **not** to receive unsolicited direct marketing calls.

So, I advise you to check your list of companies before you pick up the phone.

I have listed the CTPS website on the resources page at the back of the book.

If you buy leads, most companies will have done this step for you.

A Quick Checklist:

- ✓ We have our script
- ✓ We have an idea of what possible outcomes to expect
- ✓ We have our CRM
- ✓ We have our leads

However, we are still missing one last thing:

Our Toolkit!

DO NOT PICK UP THE PHONE WITHOUT THIS IN PLACE!

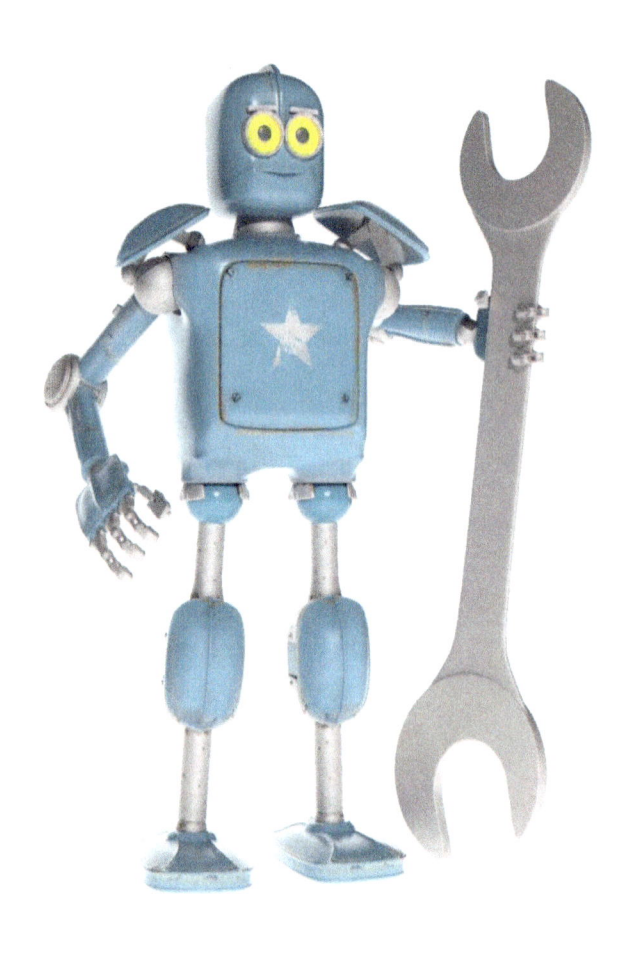

STEP 11
YOUR TOOLKIT

Before we can pick up the phone; let's talk about your "phone-ready" marketing materials.

Your marketing materials play a huge role in supporting your call and lending weight to your story. You must have your toolkit at the ready for anyone who wants additional information about your services/offering.

Your kit should include the following:

- An up-to-date, well maintained and easy to navigate website
- A professional business email address - name@thecompanyimcallingfrom.com
- A follow-up email template
- Examples of your work: This could be pdf case studies, links to case studies, or anything you feel showcases your work/ideas. For example, a designer might

want to include links to work they are proud of. (You may not have this yet, so just use your website).
- Quotes from clients/customers
- Social Media - Twitter, Instagram, Facebook, Pinterest, Linked In etc. Whatever is relevant to your business
- A rate card, if applicable

This kit is essential when you cold call because many people will not agree to your **Why** straight away. Most people like to have a look at what you do before they commit.

Your follow up email needs to be concise and reflect what you've said on the phone. Go back to your sentence and create something around that.

We all receive emails that we ignore, but you are sending a follow-up to your previous conversation. So, if the conversation has gone well, it is more likely to be read.

Just remember to keep the email concise. People do not tend to read long emails.

On the following page is an email template you could personalise.

EMAIL EXAMPLE:

Re: Your Company name & anything you think will grab attention

Dear

Thank you for your time today *(personalise this if anything else happened on your call)*. As promised, here are further details regarding *(Your Company Name)*.

As I mentioned on the phone today, we are (**SAY WHAT YOU DO**)

I've attached examples of our work/here is a link to my work/YouTube Channel – **whatever you feel is relevant to your company and what you think would be the right thing to showcase you.**

You can also visit our website: …………………………….

(If you have any insight into the company and why you feel you can benefit them, then put that here.)

If you have any questions or would like to arrange (YOUR WHY), please do not hesitate to drop me a line or call me on (*phone number or email address. Tailor this sentence to match your **WHY**).

I look forward to speaking again soon. (Or as promised, I will give you a call on...)

Kind regards

In your signature include any social media links, your logo, email and telephone number.

STEP 12
WHAT MAKES A GOOD CALL?

*B*efore we dive in, it's helpful to look at what makes a good call and the techniques you need to feel confident on the phone.

A good call flows, we feel connected to the person we're speaking to, and we're not left feeling like we've just had an ear battering!

To think about what makes a good call, we must consider what makes a bad one.

Thinking about your reactions will help you become brilliant at picking up the phone and chatting to the people you want to speak with. (I say with, not at or to!)

So, take a moment and mull over the cold calls you've ever received.

- How did they make you feel?
- How did you react?
- Were you talked at?
- Did you feel as though you were listened to?
- Was a connection made?
- Did you feel rubbed up the wrong way?
- Did you buy into whatever the person wanted from you?
- Did you wish you had never picked up the phone in the first place?
- What was their voice like? Was it too slick and sounding too rehearsed? Or did they sound genuine?
- Was there background noise?
- Did the call sound professional?
- Did you feel that you were just a number on a long, long, long list?

Drawing on your own experiences will enable you to walk in the shoes of the person you're calling.

We know how we react, what irritates us, and similarly what makes us warm to a person. Chances are that the person you're calling may well feel the same. They are human, after all!

My next point is put succinctly in the quote below:

"Listening is an art that requires attention over talent, spirit over ego, others over self. **– Dean Jackson**

To become good at using the phone, you have to listen, listen, and listen some more.

Take a deep breath and get over yourself. Leave your ego at the door. The call is not about what you want. It is about the person you call and whether what you offer can benefit them, **NOT** how they can help you.

In my experience, the best calls have been where I have said very little at all. Instead, I've laid out my wares, something resonates, and I listen as the spark of interest starts to ignite.

We are trying to have a conversation with someone, not just offload our agenda. Let the person know that you might potentially be of use to them. Give them space and room to talk. You might even learn a thing or two if you truly listen.

Before I make my calls, I imagine that each one is a precious seed. The seed needs care and attention to blossom and to reach its full potential. Treat each call in this way, and your new business will bloom.

Bear in mind the following:

- The call is more memorable for them if they do more of the talking.
- Ask yourself, how many times does your mind wander off when you are being talked at?
- Conversations are more memorable if there are two sides to them.

However, listening starts before you even begin to speak.

When you first connect:

- Listen to their tone of voice. Do they sound anxious, stressed, or distracted?
- What background noises do you hear? Do they sound like they are on a train? Are they working from home with children in the background?

Those few short moments set the tone of the call and your reaction to them. If you react appropriately to what you hear, you will have created a real connection.

Don't be afraid to listen to your gut. If it sounds like they are up to their eyes in chaos, then work that into your conversation, don't just launch into your script. Instead, react to the situation like the human that you are!

Even if it means saying, *"I'm sorry, you sound busy, should I call you another time?"*

You will have listened first and put them first, a vital step in building good relationships on the phone.

I invite you to think about other aspects of calls or conversations you've had that have worked for you. That makes you feel connected, listened to and cared about. I came across the following quote:

"Sincerity can actually be heard in the voice. It conveys a sense of trust, compassion, friendliness, approachability, and authority...if you're sincere, you'll be believable". - www.Voices.com

Whatever it is you are calling about, you must do it with integrity and honesty.

The way to be an excellent cold-caller is to care about what you're talking about and respect the time of the person you are calling. Again, I cannot stress this enough; the call is not about you but them. Be mindful of the fact that you are interrupting their day and asking for their time.

- Do not take the energy from the last call into the next one.
- Each call is individual.
- Listen, Talk and Listen some more
- Do Not Be Pushy

We are going for classy and sophisticated. Upbeat and in control. If you believe in what you are talking about, then let the work speak for itself. If you push your ideas onto the person you call, you will have them running in the opposite direction.

Keep it light, friendly and courteous and again, let your work, product, service, whatever it is that you do speak for itself!

Own Your Slip-Ups & Mistakes

If you make a mistake, stumble or trip over your words, then just own it. Laugh and say what's on your mind. For example:

> ***"Gosh, sorry, my mouth is just not in gear with my brain today."***

You're more likely to get a good response because, well, we've all been there!

Be as natural as you can be, and it will make you more relatable than simply reeling off your script.

Energy

When I talk about energy, I'm referring to the energy of the call. You may have just had a fantastic conversation with someone bubbly and lively, and you've got your YES, and you are riding high. You pick up the phone, still feeling euphoric, and all your attention is on how YOU feel. You don't notice things like tone of voice, background noises, and you dive in with full force.

This approach can jeopardise your potential relationship with the next person because you have forgotten the fundamental rule that the person you are speaking to comes first.

After every conversation, take a breath and reset yourself so that your energy is constant, and you can keep your focus on who you are calling. By all means, jump up and down, run around the room, whoop a bit. I know I do, and when you've calmed down, come back to the phone and get those listening ears back in tune.

The same goes when you've had a negative call. Just shake it off. I have to be honest and say that I've rarely had unpleasant calls in all my years of calling. If you stay polite and respond to the person you speak to, you'll find that you won't have many unpleasant calls.

KEY POINTS TO MAKING A GOOD CALL

- Be sincere
- Believe in your work
- Leave your ego at the door
- The call is not about you
- Create space for the other person to speak
- Do not be pushy
- Let your work speak for itself
- Less is more
- Treat each call as precious
- LISTEN, LISTEN, LISTEN
- Do not take the energy from one call to another
- Own your stumbles
- Ask Open Questions. For example - When are you reviewing? When would be a good time to call? How does your review process work?

A QUICK CHECK

- ✓ We have our script
- ✓ We have an idea of what possible outcomes to expect
- ✓ We have our CRM
- ✓ We have our leads
- ✓ We have our toolkit!
- ✓ We know what makes a good call

Thus, leading us swiftly onto the last part of our journey. Vocal and mental preparation for that first call.

STEP 13
HOW TO SAY IT

Your voice is your biggest asset when you are on the phone. It is, after all, the first thing a person hears.

We all make snap decisions about people when we first meet them, and the same thing happens when you hear a voice at the end of the line.

Think about how you respond to voices:

- Is the voice warm?
- Does it grate on your nerves?

- Does it sound genuine?
- Do you want to keep talking to the owner of this voice?
- Is it insincere and false sounding?

What we say is very important, but **how** we say it also has to be considered.

When my son was little, he would not eat anything unless it was in a bread roll. Fish cakes, mince, fish fingers, sausages, bananas, you name it, it had to be in a roll. If you offered any of these items in any other way, he would simply refuse to eat them.

My point being is that the way you present information (your **What**) is fundamental. The only way you can present your information on the phone is with your voice.

I think my calling success is because I like my voice, and I feel very comfortable speaking. I'm not weighed down by wondering whether my voice will work or not, so I have a freedom when I communicate.

I started out as a singer/actor, and the skills I learned have held me in good stead. I also trained as a Voicegym instructor with the late Angela Lewis and learned valuable techniques to connect with my voice.

For me, a good "telephone" voice will not be monotonous, too fast or too slow, too high or too low. It will be clear, warm, rhythmic, energetic, engaging and sincere. Your voice should convey and reflect your thoughts.

At the Vocal Bureau, so many people come to me because they do not like the sound of their own voice. When they hear themselves, they don't relate to the sound they make. Nerves cripple them in presentations and pitch meetings. They can't pick up the phone, and they rely solely on email to build relationships. However, voice and the ability to communicate is central to creating opportunities and building relationships.

You have to "own" your voice and understand how it works. When you speak, you want to be comfortable with the sound you are making. If you're not in control, your voice can get in the way of the thoughts you want to communicate. There is nothing more debilitating than when you are not in sync with your sound.

Pace and rhythm are other things people often have problems with, and they do not know how to play with the tempo and pitch of their speech and end up sounding monotonous and dull. To help, you can read poems to music in varying tempos to help you connect with the musicality which lies within good speech.

These are common issues I come across:

- People feel that they sound too young
- There are ongoing speech and voice issues
- Voice lacking charisma and charm and lacking pitch and rhythm
- Speech issues arise when people are nervous
- People simply freeze up when it comes to speaking
- People talk too fast and "gabble"
- Having a constant frog in the throat and are constantly clearing it
- People complain that their voice just doesn't feel like theirs
- Frequent voice loss, vocally fatigued at the end of a presentation, pitch or meeting

If any of this resonates, then I recommend looking into vocal coaching. As it so happens, I run a tailored fundamental voice programme to help people unlock their vocal potential. You can visit my website: www.thevocalbureau.com/Businesses

However, there are things you can do right now.

VOCAL CARE

Voice Warm-ups – There are plenty of voice exercises on YouTube and vocal coaches offering tuition. As I have already mentioned, I am a vocal coach, so you can always drop me a line, and we can talk about your individual vocal needs and how I can help.

Warm up your neck and shoulders. You could try neck care with Adrienne. Visit her yoga channel on YouTube.

Stay hydrated by drinking plenty of water (room temperature). Also, reduce your coffee, tea and fizzy drinks as these can cause dehydration. Replace teas and coffee with herbal teas instead.

Be mindful of your posture, and don't slouch in your chair when you are on the phone. You can stand up or sit on an ergonomic chair or yoga ball. If you suffer from neck pain, stiff shoulders, sore back, etc., invest some time in yourself and find a cranial osteopath or chiropractor.

Use a headset to prevent neck strain, and don't sit with the phone in the crook of your neck whilst you do your calling.

Steam your throat to keep your voice in tip-top condition. Take a bowl of boiling water, place a towel over your head and breathe in the steam. Or get fancy and buy a facial steamer. Do not add anything to the water like eucalyptus, as this could be drying.

Acid reflux can be a problem for voice users as it can affect the voice leaving you hoarse. If you suspect that you have acid reflux and have voice problems, visit your GP or alternative healthcare provider.

Dentistry – look after your teeth. Your teeth and jaw alignment have an enormous impact on your vocal health. If you have dental or bite issues, it is worth visiting your dentist for advice. Find a holistic dentist/orthodontist who will understand the connections between teeth and voice.

If you have any voice concerns, you can contact me via - www.thevocalbureau.com

STEP 14
MENTAL PREPARATION

*B*efore you make each call make sure you are mentally prepared. You need your head in the game with your eyes on the prize!

Your mindset plays a big part in how your calling will go. If you come to it with dread and a lack of enthusiasm, this negativity will show through in your calls, and people will respond to the way you sound. (As I mentioned, your thoughts will colour your voice).

Before I start my calling day, my affirmation is that I know I will have a good day. I will find a good opportunity, and I will have good conversations. I also make sure that I have beautiful things to look at; photos of sunsets, warm beaches, an eagle flying, that sort of thing. I also love my home office/workspace, and this reflects in my voice.

Your mood will drive the calling day. So, get positive and get into a "Can Do" attitude.

- Visualise how your day is going to go
- Say a positive affirmation in your head or out loud
- Smile and be sincere in your thoughts. A smile lifts the voice but does not mask the intention.
- Banish the dread and enjoy the challenge.
- Approach each call with hopeful expectancy.
- Have your diary open with the expectation of filling it with new opportunities

If you find yourself in an energy slump, get up and walk about, jog on the spot, get some fresh air, have a break, do something positive to re-energise your mind and voice.

If you lack motivation at the start of your calling session, try to remember why you are calling:

- Do you have a bigger picture?
- Are you living your Ikigai?
- What will building your business mean to you, your family, your life?
- What are your hopes and dreams?

Use this to help you focus on the task at hand and find the inspiration you need to get calling time after time after time.

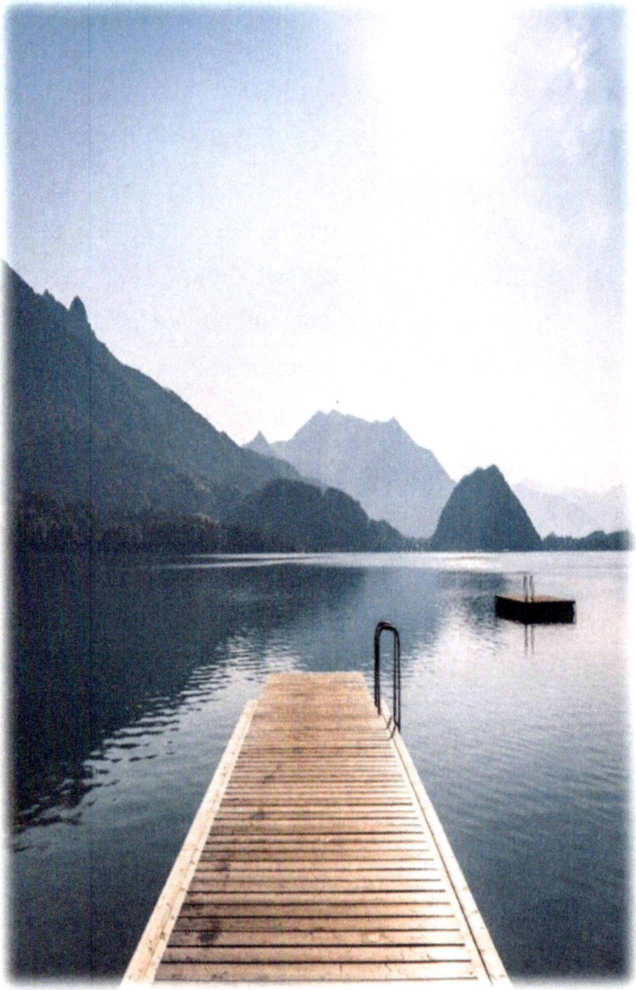

STEP 15
YOUR FIRST CALL & BEYOND

You are now ready to start your new business calling. Yippee, I hear you all cry!

As always, here is a quick checklist before you dive in:

- Wipe the sweat from your brow!
- Database open
- Script at hand
- Email template and toolkit ready
- Smile and keep pleasant thoughts in your head, and know that it's not enough just to smile. The smile needs to come from a place or sincerity for it to colour your voice.
- Visualise that the day ahead is going to be productive
- Open your website if it inspires you.
- A pleasant work environment.
- A relaxed attitude.
- Warm up your voice.

- Set your intention to have good conversations.
- Take breaks as and when you need them.
- Don't let rejections get you down. Just move on.
- Be diligent with your note keeping.
- Follow up with any requests immediately!
- Do not take the energy from the last call into the next one. Each call is individual.
- LISTEN, LISTEN, LISTEN
- Enjoy yourself
- You've Got This!
- **Happy Calling!**

ARGHHHHH! NOW WHAT?

So, you've just made your call, and now the new business development really starts.

The follow-up and how you conduct yourself after you've called **IS AS IMPORTANT AS THE CALL ITSELF!**

I know I don't need to shout, but I'm going to anyway because this step is **CRUCIAL!**

Here is my follow-up checklist:

- ✓ **HAVE YOUR FOLLOW-UP EMAIL READY TO GO**

Having your email template to hand will help your calling day go more smoothly, make you look efficient and help keep you in the mind of the person you have just spoken with.

- ✓ **SEND YOUR FOLLOW-UP EMAIL IMMEDIATELY**

With any call you make, it is essential to follow up with the email you promised to send, the materials you mentioned or the diary confirmation for that meeting.

Remember - Just because you have put the phone down does not mean your call is over!

You have to do whatever you said you were going to do and do it **IMMEDIATELY!** (Sorry for shouting again)

Imagine that you are still on the call even after you've hung up and action everything you said you would do. The energy of the call is still alive, so keep it positive and complete it correctly.

Your goal is to stay in someone's mind enough so that when you call them again, they remember you, or at least have a recollection of your previous call.

Sending the materials hours later is not going to make a good impression. You are barely in their mind when they've put the phone down, so if you can have your email lined up and ping it into their inbox within a few minutes, referencing the call you just had, you have more chance of building a rapport and achieving your **Why**.

✓ **DO NOT FORGET TO UPDATE YOUR CRM**

Until you have done your admin, you cannot pick up the phone to the next person.

✓ **FIND A GENUINE REASON TO STAY IN TOUCH**

It's important to stay in touch with the people you have connected with. Keep your eyes and ears open and if you see anything that might give you a reason to call and have a genuine conversation, then pick up the phone!

Follow this system for every call, and you will soon have a pipeline of opportunities for the short and long term.

TROUBLESHOOTING

So, you've done everything by the book, but it's just not working! You've spent hours, weeks, even months calling and still nothing seems to be happening.

Do not pull your hair out. Instead, take a deep breath and step back.

Be as objective as you can be and ask yourself the following questions:

- Is your **WHO** and **WHAT** sentence correct?
- Revisit who you are and what you do.
- Are you concise enough? Is there waffle going on?
- Perhaps try your script out on friends and family and see whether it flows?
- Is what you do very visual or too complex, to sum up in two sentences? Could you send something via email or in the post first and follow it up with a call?
- Are you in a competitive field?

- Can you offer additional value that your competitors can't?
- Can you add more weight to your call by name dropping or referring to live work/ press coverage etc.
- Is your **Why** clear enough? Do you get to the point of the call quickly? What is the purpose of your call? Is there too much waffle?
- Are you targeting the right sector?
- Are you talking to the right people within the right sector?
- Is your follow-up email good enough?
- Are you immediately following up on your calls with the materials

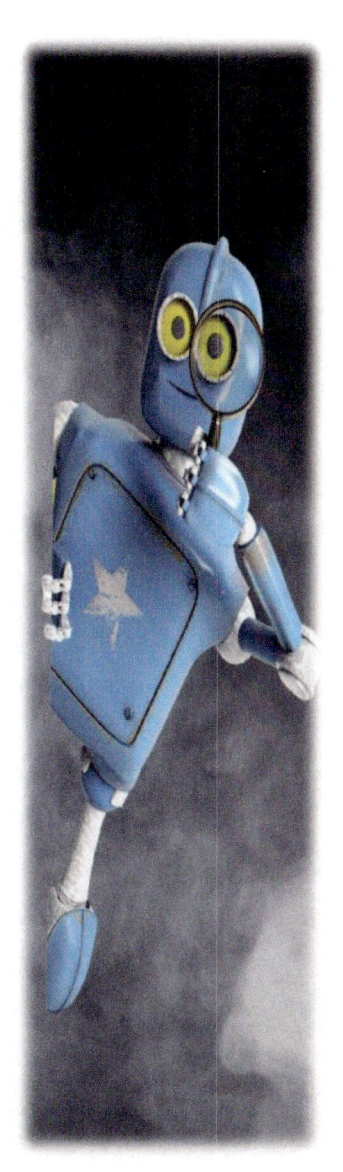

you said you would send?
- Are your marketing materials good enough? Do they look professional and well presented?
- Are you following up your initial calls with your follow up calls?
- Are you calling when you said you would, or are you waiting for them to get back to you? (It does happen, but often, people need a nudge)
- Assess what is going on in the world around your sector and in general, i.e., pandemics and lockdowns! Is there anything that could be hampering your efforts?
- Are you blowing your own trumpet enough? Don't be backwards in mentioning live, memorable, and current work
- Try different calling windows. Maybe you are calling first thing on a Monday and just not getting through to anyone because they are taking meetings. Vary the times you call and observe whether there are better times than others for the sector you are working with.
- Is your phone/headphone clear? Are you calling from your mobile, landline or

computer, is there distracting background noise?
- Are you talking or listening? Remember, your priority is to get them to talk more than you.
- Are you enjoying your phone experience?
- Are you relaxed?
- Do you believe in what you are saying?
- Do you feel connected to your voice? Remember that what you are thinking will influence how you sound. Your thoughts colour your voice.

If all else fails, you may need to call in additional support to help see where the problem lies.

There are many consultants out there, or you could reach out and contact me:

www.thevocalbureau.com/contact-us

CONCLUSION

I hope you've enjoyed our journey into the wonderful world of cold-calling and have come away with a spring in your step, a sense of purpose and above all, the belief that you can create your own new business opportunities.

People, more than ever, want to have good conversations and make real connections.

Remember to be honest and open and love what you do and who you do it for.

Follow the steps, keep the faith and develop patience.

Be your own superhero, build your business and create your own opportunities.

"Until you spread your wings, you will have no idea how far you can fly."

– Unknown

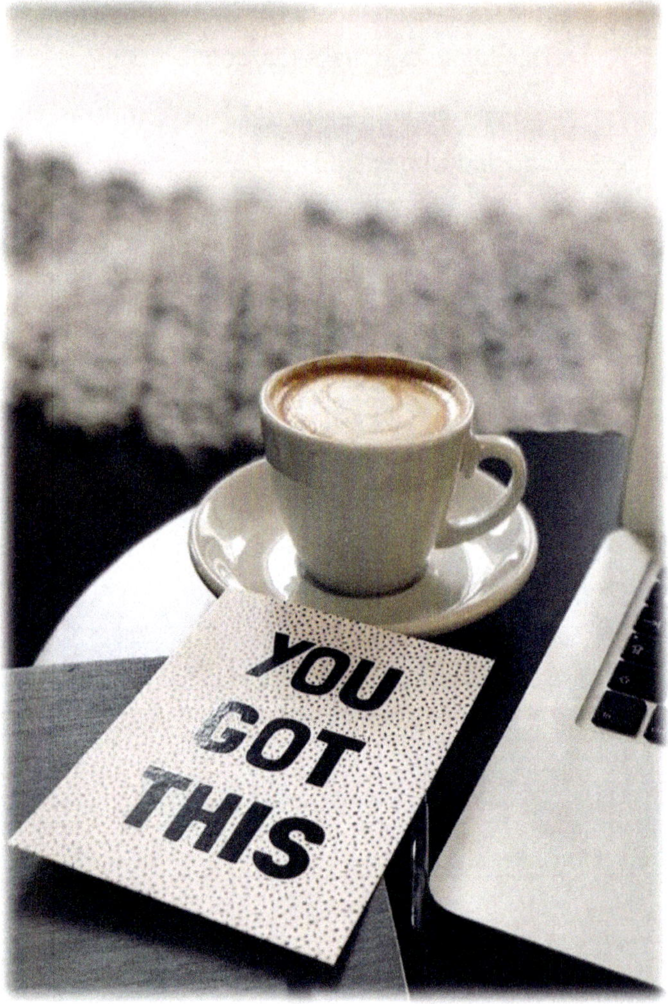
YOU
GOT
THIS

SCRIPT TEMPLATE

ADDRESS:

NAME:

EMAIL:

PHONE:

WEB ADDRESS:

Good Morning/ Afternoon could I speak to

My name is

and I am calling from

We're

and work with

I was hoping to arrange

IF YES – Perfect. Can I take your email address and I will send you a diary invite (or whatever you have agreed upon) and a link to our website

If NO/Maybe then ask open questions -

When, Why, How, What

RESOURCES

USEFUL LINKS

The Vocal Bureau - www.thevocalbureau.com

Email me: simone@thevocalbureau.com

For Beautiful Designs –

https://www.facebook.com/MelliMDesigns

LEADS

www.electricmarketing.co.uk

Free CTPS Checker | Electric Marketing

ALF Insight | Agency New Business

www.linkedin.com

Telephone Preference Service - (ctpsonline.org.uk)

CRM SYSTEMS

www.salesforce.com

www.thehubspot.com

www.goldmine.com

www.pipedrive.com

OVERALL HEALTH & WELLBEING

VoiceGym - www.voicegym.co.uk

The Complementary Medical Association

www.the-cma.org.uk

Dr Peter Glidden – MD Naturopath

https://www.riseupintohealth.com

https://riseupintohealth.com/?via=simone

The British Voice Association

https://www.britishvoiceassociation.org.uk

Yoga With Adrienne – YouTube

The Daily Om – Courses

www.dailyom.com/cgi-bin/courses/courses.cgi

Ikigai: The Japanese secret to a long and happy life - By Hector Garcia & Francesc Miralles

THE HEALING POINT: Your step-by-step guide to ketogenic wellness – By James Lilley

EQUIPMENT

Yoga Ball – For posture and voice work

Theraband - For Stretching & Voice Work

Facial Steamer

Notebooks for scribbling ideas:

www.magictreebooks.co.uk

To Do List

About The Author

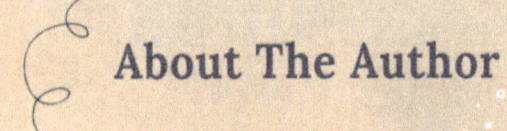

Simone has always loved to talk and has created a path for herself centred around voice.

With a Combined Honours Degree in English Literature & Music from The University of Southampton, Postgraduate Diploma & LRAM in Vocal Studies, from The Royal Academy of Music and a VoiceGym Practitioner, she has worked as a voice coach for over 20 years.

Her cold-calling experience stemmed from running new business and marketing for The Voice Gym in Southampton. She found she loved being on the phone building relationships with potential clients.

This led to her working with companies from across the marketing services sector, both B2B & B2C. Simone has been a successful new business consultant for over 20 years.

To connect her skills and experience, The Vocal Bureau was born. She helps individuals and companies learn what to say, how to say it and whom to say it to.

www.thevocalbureau.com

THANK YOU FOR READING.

If you enjoyed the journey please feel free to give a big thumbs-up on Amazon.

Thank you!

www.thevocalbureau.com

Printed in Great Britain
by Amazon